Books by David Imburgia

POETRY
Ripples (2016)
Getting Grip (2020)

GETTING GRIP

DAVID IMBURGIA

Copyright ©2020 David Imburgia

All rights reserved. No part of this book may be used, reproduced or transmitted in any form or by any means, electronic, mechanical, photocopying, recording or otherwise, without the prior written consent of the publisher.

Poems.
ISBN: 978-0-578-81084-3
Published by Village Books

First Edition.
Bellingham, Washington

PREFACE

My poems have been to an adventure to explore. I have loved the surprises. I embraced the adventures of learning, family, friends, acceptance of change, and heartbreak. I've crossed continents for adventure. It has filled me with a well of wonder.

Some of life's twists have turned out to be of good fortune. More to learn. The selective service draft of 1968 was a major twist, that eventually led me to explore college. At the time, I was busy raising a son, working a job, and attending school full time. Then suddenly poetry was creeping up my sleeve, prompting me to put my thoughts to paper.

I did not imagine the doors that would open by sharing art, our most precious gift. So many of my own doors were so important to open. I sent me and I followed. The grand parade leads me on to the next adventure.

IN GRATITUDE

First and foremost, thank you to my wife, Celie, who is a steady support and friend for my art and life. I am also grateful to my brother, Dan, whose art is shown on the cover of Getting Grip, "Prayer for Owen Meany." He is also a fine poet. I could not imagine this book coming to birth so well without Sherry Matthews, a fine editor and designer. Of course, many others deserve appreciation... John Green, Marion Brodhagen, Katie Harwood, David B., Carla... my sincere appreciation to all!

Getting Grip

Connections 1
   Neruda's Credo 3
   Appointments 5
   Cutthroats 7
   Separation 9
   Many Years 11
   To Lose A Thing 15
   Bonded 17
   Our Four Points 19
   Daylight Savings 21
   Cardinal Singer 23
   Gentle Eyes 25
   Let Me 27
   Gifting 29
   Glass 31
   The Romantics 33
   You and Me, Finally 37

Courage 39
   The Angels 41
   Peacemonger 43
   Caregiver 45
   Diamond Peak 47
   To Know the Right 49

Passages 51
   Breathless 53
   Three Lines 55
   Virus 57
   Take Out 59
   Getting Grip 61
   Emergency Rooms 63
   Feeding the Chimera 65
   Poet's Journey 69
   The Local Tribe 71
   Weathering 73
   Cardinal Center Right 75
   Gran Milonga 77
   Humans — From The Feline Guide 79
   Factory Job 81
   Weather Report 83
   Two Days 85
   Tai Chi 87
   Manzanita Rush — The Explorers 89
   The Clockmaker 91
   Passing Pigeons 93
   Broken Down 95

- Questions in Bottles 97
  - Questions in a Bottle 99
  - Trickle Down 101
  - Time Machine 103
  - Notre-Dame de Paris 105
  - Baptism 107
  - How Would I Paint? 109
  - The Smile 111
- Role Play 113
  - Current Affairs 115
  - Black or White 117
  - Safety 119
  - The Sky is Falling 121
  - Dialogue 123
  - Everyday Justice 125
  - Fixing the System 127
  - Addicted to Salvation 129
  - God Bless 131
  - The Perfect Poem 133
- Star Trails 135
  - Heaven 137
  - Hell 139
  - Purgatory 141
  - Katabatic 143
  - Rippling 145
  - Star Trails 147
  - Color Rising 149
  - Galileo Galilei 151
  - Siblings 153
  - Your Dust 155
  - Moonrise 157
  - Moonlight 161
  - The Ambered Phoenix 163
  - Give Us Your Poor 165
- The Border 167
  - At the Border 169
  - Passages 171
  - Sonriendo 173
  - Home of the Brave 177

Connections

NERUDA'S CREDO

My children,
    I did not tell you
        about death
so you could live forever.

I did not tell you
    about crime and hate
        so you would not fear.
    War is not forgotten by me,
        but unlearned by you,
    so you could rejoice
    without indignant fury,
        without cruelty.

Now you are elders
    older than I was then,
    and I ask for forgiveness
        knowing my own death
        not as a crime,
    knowing my love
        as antidote of fear.

Righteous, we can be pawns
without our own minds.
Righteous, we are cruel and
        less than we can be.

My children forgive me -
    I gave you everything
    when there was nothing,
    and nothing could grow on nothing.
        Everything is substance
    or absence of substance.

We know only
    that all things combine, change
and become dissolute.
    And I am creation of circumstance
    and creator of circumstance.
        A morality play
    a tragedy perhaps
    for the making of you.

Politics and religion
    are your shackles and mine
    until I write these words
    until you read.
All is transformed by reason
    tempered by emotion.

This is the excuse of an apostle
to follow you
    as you follow me.
And now you may teach your children
    a new way to play.

APPOINTMENTS

These dates we most need
to keep, seem to keep us,

to give us content
between the lines,
an inner working
to a vast clock.

We meet appointments.
We miss them.
Postpone, cancel,
pursue, and avoid them.

We are guilty for them
and relieved.
Even terrified
or humiliated.

We set them in place
as wardens, to
enforce a purpose
for our days.

We need to know
someone is waiting for us.

CUTTHROATS

The river runs wild at the bridge.
Water whips drowned rocks.
Baldheaded boulders peek from pools
rich in glacial silt and
awash in schools of cutthroats.

Our fishing lines snake forked tongues,
darting into promising pools.
Green moss slicks our footing.
I warn Bryan. He is already in up to his knees
like a prophet answering praise.

My line snaps and lays a single finger
where I point. The cutthroats see it arrive
and laugh back. I've caught a fly.
I probe at a sudden anger.

Bryan is hungry. Where are the fish?
When do we eat? How long must we stay?
Strikes nibble at my answers.
Father and Son today. Why doesn't he bite?
Quiet. I work it out on the fish.

My fly rod is tense and rigid, lined with loops,
hung with twisted wire. A weapon.
I'm beating the nature out of it.

Bryan gathers stones. His pockets bulge
like chipmunk cheeks. A feather
from an eagle or a sparrow
tucks over one ear like a writing quill.

The sun burns a message into my brow.
I've forgotten my hat. My feet are wet.
The cutthroats swim cool and safe.
Bryan wets a tree. Picks mushrooms.
Snaps sticks into Viking fragments and frees them.

He skips flats of shale
over the roof of pools where my patience waits.
Now it's too late. The fish know us by name.
I help Bryan fill the river
with a barrage of flat skipping stones.

Later he is asleep on his seat.
The county road is not well kept.
I fight the curves for awhile,
then at a straightaway I check his face.
A smile lifts the corner of his lips.
A gum wrapper nests in the clutch of his hand.

River water and mud stiffen his jeans.
I see leaves loosen from branches then
like brittle canoes float downstream.
Pyrite pebbles escape through pocket holes.
Fishing lines snag in trees.

Fathers impatiently bend at the knees
wondering over good fishing trips and memories.
Wet rocks. Loud water. Wise fish.

SEPARATION

The dog sleeps on the bed now
It's not the same
He snores
He uses all of your space
Your pillow I keep special

MANY YEARS

I love your body
as I love youth.
I no longer fear youth
nor can I respect it,
the biggest thief
inflicting us all
with life's inevitable surprise.

Be with me this short while.
I promise to honor you
when you have learned, when
you have pulled the marrow
of logic through the thin teeth of Hebron
and before the mirrors of days
turn bright with promises and lies.

As for me
I'm stuck in here
for now.
I test the doors and locks
remaining patient, like a hare
with a fox on the prowl.
The locks are confirmed.
They will fail.

I will love your youth, the body
of geometry and the soft bones
so easy to curl into fist or embrace.

I will love with you
your choices, the arrows
fletched with innocence,
the errors of days turned
to a joy of satisfaction.
These, I must release.

Release me, and you are free.
Or stay and contain me
but you must be free.
Invitation offers one love

like the very last love
while good fortune emerges
as benevolent accomplice of
the best angels of intent.

Yet, some may flee
and be missed by the point,
but others will comprehend
how we are all one,
the family of man
the animal kingdom
the choices of the spirit
the divineness of comedy
the comedy of tragedy.

We want to believe
it is not all undone with
the currency of changing faces,
or the crypts
of bones and dreams.
Ah, Renaissance!
Cross the narrow line
of ambivalence.
Enlightenment of love
inflict me once again.

Leave me injustice,
and leave me the revenge
of the sparrow slain
by youth's vast ignorance.

This is a love song,
not a thief in the market
or a pilgrimage to Portugal
but one last thought to barter.

That many years from now,
from my unlocked doors
to your doors and windows,
many, many years,

and if you remember me
as you lie down in turn,
all will seem
as only yesterday.

TO LOSE A THING

To lose a thing and then let go
allows something else in its place
or at least leaves us more free.

In our nature,
we struggle to be satisfied.
How else could we be?

We are better when we change
with grace, when we are moving
believing we are improving.

There are mountains that walk,
their knees bent and strong.
They learn all they need by going slow.

Consider how we sort
and choose and believe.
We make adjustments to fit

what we require,
making excuses for the inconvenient.
It can be hard work

to look for what is gained.
Something is gone, you are gone
I will go too, all lost, all changed.

Maybe it is finally all miracles,
all the time, all miracles
all coming our way.

Just as well.
Snuggle up.
Watch the parade.

BONDED

My brother's heart is not perfect—
It has its own unnatural rhythm
to challenge the drumbeat
of his rapid mind.

His heart mocks an internal cadence.
It flutters like an electric current
with crossed wires,
or a memory stored
then retrieved in erratic bits.

But his mind is clear
and his faith in place

though lately he's not
taking as many chances.
He munches hemp cookies
and drives the speed limit.

He criticizes philosophers or politicians
for any mimic comments
on business-as-usual
or holy mortality.

I am surprised at our intersections,
having travelled such separate roads.
But his path is well-worn, and
he is no more conflicted than you or I.
Though we may diverge on the importance of designs
and possible immortalities.

I admire his gentle disagreements.
His mind is woven with threads of ideals.
His hands are kind and give gifts of art.
He teaches as he learns.

I stammer my hope
that he lives both
our versions of forever.

OUR FOUR POINTS

                Before you were here

        What you meant   While you were near

              When you went

DAYLIGHT SAVINGS

There is a certain river,
a stream of light, in tides
that often sneaks into
northern latitudes in January.

We hurry to gather what we can.
We use all our containers,
even take off our shirts to fill them
brimming with the silvers, the golds,

and platinum of afternoons
before the return of long winter night.
We save what we can.
No matter, it runs out too soon,

and we are left muttering for June.
We act as if it never ends,
the fulcrum upon which this
January light abruptly bends.

Imagine we could send some forward
some glimmers saved from our surprise
like an anonymous gift to
a winter-weary northerner.

But we can't send light
or weigh it against the mystery of time.
It teases and tears the fabric then
runs through us, daylight into night.

CARDINAL SINGER

Cardinal singer
a flame, you flicker
        through your wood,
        lighting our world.

Your bold song
        and embered feathers
of brilliant color
        are glorious but brief.

Crows and hawks target you.
You earn
        a gallant compensation
for a light so quickly flared.

Against the sky
or the woodland
you are forever framed
        in my memory held.

GENTLE EYES

Your gentle eyes
Open in kiss
Wide in passion
Seek spirit
Taste soul
Speak in silence
Hint at Coyote
Miss nothing
Reflect everything
Take me in
Know my story
Beginning and end.

LET ME

Let me make memories of us
before we begin.

We could spend a few coins on
surprises and dinners,
and dependable bottles of wine.
We might make friends
and lovers of each other
by knowing what we learn.

Certain of only what may come,
we may be fortune's children
and have some time for play.

It's all a chance,
a dime on the floor,
the music and more,
the mix of motive and time.

I could have come this way
an hour later, or a day,
and missed you by a mile.

This way, we embrace for days.
I hold you this way, then that,
until we move along again
while only a trace remains.

Memories are like fog, they shift-shape
to fill a space, leave a thought or a face.

Memories will make us cry
or wonder why we don't.

GIFTING

All through childhood
Don't we love the gifts we receive?

Memories come alive for the tinsel and joy
in the celebration of ourselves.

Birthday or Christmas, no matter
even unexpected guilt toys,

we take them all.
Expectations are sometime satisfied.

Eventually we are taught to handmake
cards to give to our mothers in token.

But it is only with passing years
we might be surprised in return,

with the greater gift than things
in the discovery

to have love we have given
be cherished.

GLASS

Your second glance asked
Why I looked away
from the smile you offered

Your gaze registered
after the moment had passed
    then felt like the electric touch of a child
    on the heaving flanks of a nervous stallion.

But our eyes confused the question
    so earnestly posed, indelibly impressed
    in mystery between us.
I realized too late but looked again.

Did you see it then?

Like a glass pane placed between us,
an invisible but final divider,
    marked now by hints
     of salty haloed rings,
    like drops of rain
after heat has dried them small.

THE ROMANTICS

Love takes our truths
and shapes them believable.

It's not hard.
We believe what we choose

as old age whispers, whispers
in everyone's closet.

Time compresses,
vanishing into memories.

We keep photo albums
but they are invisible, locked

away in pretense.
Our names become precious.

We say words to hear voices.
Truths become legends and

the memories lose patience, lose place,
become monasteries.

There is much to pray for
but darkness does not find us on our knees.
.
We watch winter stars.
We love winter breath.

There is promise still in
the shapeshifting of hope.

Time does not pass into a river,
it is we who enter the flow again

and again, to say it is not so
to prove the futility of

French philosophy and the rosary
of rote passage, the journey

East, the new sun, the new sun
the repeat of day and delight

and the necessity
the carousel delivers,

not a rotation, but a surprise
that old friends will come again

like arisen family, like spirits
of children finding children

clasped to the hearts of mothers
suckling the breasts of fame and

ignorant of all other purpose.
Oh, this is a vague path,

the essence of passage from
one light, one love, one belief.

The passage from love of me
to love of you.

The great compassion and the
imminent wonder of release;

All things run together,
all substance and non-substance,

all love and hate come to matter.
And we hold our truths

as Truths, as icons of belief
carried as children

to children, our love
as reason enough;

All there will be
all there was

and all that is
required.

YOU AND ME, FINALLY

Trees filter
the morning sun
Greening the world.

Color and silhouettes
Filter through to us
As we sit below.

We listen.
Both of us aware how
Important are your hands.

The leaves rustle.
A breeze drifts.
The slow morning warms.

Blackbirds and warblers
Flicker through the canopy.
They sing

As they have forever
But this morning
They sing for you and me.

Courage

THE ANGELS

> Nothing was more important to us
> than our damn helicopters. We hated them.
> But we loved them.
> —anonymous, Vietnam, 1968

Our Angels come for us
when we are wounded,
when we are in pain.

Our Angels come for us
with a clatter of wings and dust,
as if joyous to find us.

Our Angels, our Hueys, arrive late
but they have suffered also.
The Angels have their own beauty.

We have with us the wounded
the dying, and the dead.
The Angels take them in

and we are relieved
of the terrible guilt and anger.
We are relieved of the duty

and we love the Angels
even as we need them.
Our sins recede in Angel wind.

Our Angels, these mechanical Hueys
have come to relieve us of being alone
and to lift our fear.

Our Angels carry up our terror and dreams
to take our friends, bring the mail,
and deliver us our daily ammunition.

Our Angels come for us
then lift up like prayers
carrying us to another world.

PEACEMONGER

To live the utopian dream is not the goal.
A peacemonger must be more will than fantasy,
more hope than soothsayer.

A real stoic, after all the posturing
And all the static beating of drums or the gore
Of recruiting posters done up in patriotic ink.

To give in to peace might mean to live
A life within, not in empire, busily defending
All these interests, but finding conquest

In the sustainable within.
A form of Buddhist balance and calm.
Some patience is required to make peace

Out of glory. It takes some aging and some kind
Of fortune to survive the joy
Of the quick and unexpected end.

Getting past the realization,
The religious fundament, that the outcome
In all of living is death.

Getting past the hard lesson
Of the price of having everything, to find
The joy of having less,
And giving even this away.

CAREGIVER

About care we have written
and given heroic status.

About giving we have said not enough.
Caring we understand

in the name at least of self-interest.
Giving is the same in part,

but more courageous, like believing
giving all away to inherit our own share.

Giving care is not the same.
Caregiver is more like the title

more like the resurrection
of higher ideals,

like the return of Jesus or Buddha
dressed in everyday clothes.

DIAMOND PEAK

This mountain, like a prophet
or rainmaker,
calling voltage from the sky,
tempts me still in memory.

It's a July day
offering a storm sharp and acid
while giant bolts rip the purple bruising.
The voice of thunder booms and echoes

in a steady rip and roar.
No mountain in the west
is more often struck.
I must climb, to see this shock.

A dare of the paradigm of flight,
to look through the door,
open, but a flash.
A sizzle of temptation.

Climbing Diamond Peak
testing my own youth against the storm.
Race the current to the crest!
Eyes upward to the towering clouds!

Staring into the eye.

TO KNOW THE RIGHT

> 622,000 men died in the American Civil War.
> Uncounted civilians perished.
> Walt Whitman said that future generations
> should not know of the suffering.
> Walt Whitman on this point was not correct.

It is not enough to know the names and faces,
or all the dates, that went before.
We know that the heart is within the mind,
and the mind must always be an open gate.

Even the wrong words must be unbound.
The journey into truth
is a challenge that may tear the heart.

There is this journey, and this cause, but
the road is rocks and dirt, always climbing
like a ribbon ruined by the sun.

Dragging our feet,
Led hand-in-hand by the brother who walks
near our soul,
we know not where we go.

We have belief in what the climb is for,
but the legend speaks of climbing
and also, the detail of the long fall
that will surely follow.

Every man walks alone.
We become our own history,
and mystery
of causes and effects.
Our heads are bowed, but our eyes are lifted,
though blind to the very sight we look to see.

We carry on, by days, and years,
beneath the starry banners
under which so much was promised
impossible to be delivered.
In time we grow deaf to everything
but the drum that taps our steps.

Every man—a brother.
Every leader—a brother.
The enemy—a brother.
The dead—our brothers, too.
The wounded, the lame—brothers.
The departed, the never arrived—brothers.

Every day like a repeating litany,
and the survivors
gray on blue, and all mud covered,
blue on gray, rain slicked and frozen white,
marching in slow time, marching in ranks and rows,
files and columns forever now at Carry Arms.

Youth and righteousness are here
conscripted and identified.
All choices evaporate,
even as the families disintegrate.

Though invisible in the dimming light,
like a mist in the distance, these
passing armies of sound, armies of the might
are made right, and run together,
one blood, one mother and now forever
brother beside brother.

Passages

BREATHLESS

> In memory of George Floyd Jr.
> (October 14, 1973 – May 25, 2020)

The cold curbstone
grinds my cheek
my tears run to the storm grate
Even my mother
Could not lift this pressure
Four hundred years
Holds me down
8:46 passes
But I do not notice
I never will know
My portrait lies forever still
In a distorted frame
Lighting an unexpected flame
Leaving me behind
Remembered as I cross one line
Then take all the blame
Not innocent enough to rise
Not light enough to fly
I wait still, wait for
The next penitent to kneel
I wait with millions
I wait for millions
I wait, I lie in wait
Finally, I wait
In silence
Finally
Breathless

THREE LINES

Quarantine Line
>   We each get exactly
>   Six feet of space
>   It is all we ever expected

Bad Government
>   Big government or small
>   Don't worry
>   Quality is the measure

Three Lines
>   All there is to say
>   And two lines
>   Still to go

Caring for you
>   Caring for you was not hard
>   That you valued the care
>   Was all that mattered

Short Goodbye
>   Short or sharp
>   Like a pinprick to the heart
>   Leaving the rest of the day free

Alcohol
>   Still gives me headaches
>   After the laughter
>   I keep trying

The Future
> I still play cards and games
> And I'm always at statistics
> Guessing is as good as it gets

Funerals
> There is always so much to learn
> We are never finished
> Love may blossom again

VIRUS

Suddenly there is no greeting
Eyes see everything
but each other
We pass by quickly
There is business to be done

TAKE OUT

Flavor on the run
Satisfaction's proposition
The waiter so friendly
I almost stay at the bar.

Perhaps I'd enjoy
A shift in the kitchen.
I'd be good with knives
And the cleaver.

Making up recipes
On the fly
And seasoning would
Be a measured delight.

I would make up
My own dinner
Add the special sauce
Then take it out.

GETTING GRIP

All the struggle to grab hold
Of stuff and fame and money
Comes down to legacy, or perhaps
The programming to get our share.

All the work we put into
Finding love, building things,
Planning futures, making friends
All comes down to the really hard part,

Of course. Not the holding.
It takes an insanity or courage
With feet firm to the earth,
And a heart like a feather,

A heart that gets its grip
On the important part:
It is never about what we grab
But how graceful we can be letting go.

EMERGENCY ROOMS

There is no reason to question the surgeons.
The eyes of ambulance drivers and receptionists
are less skilled at the proper disguising of panic.

Emergency rooms are always too bright—
every wound, every flow and splash
of color made all too visible.

The sounds here are muted
to urgent whispers or subdued sobs.
The staff tread the hallways in rubber soled shoes.

The two corner rooms are reserved
for the most mortal cases.
These rooms have other doors

leading deeper into trouble.
But sometimes to elevators that rise
to sunny recovery rooms

as easily as they descend into basements.
From here, there are many
halls leading to options and change.

Broken bones go to x-ray.
Children with pennies or Clorox to the pumps.
Bleeding — to the nurses' stations.

Choking? Color gone? Silent,
defiant heart? Please,
be patient.

There is always waiting.
It may be Friday night
during football season.

It may be Saturday night
after party hours
but we hope it is all in time.

Sometimes you doze.
Perhaps waking
in your own wet plastic seat.

In the dream
they found you
too peacefully sleeping.

FEEDING THE CHIMERA

Today the gardeners are putting down flowers,
setting them down in long rows, extended,
to open in order,
with the last facing the sun as it fades.

Flowers do not go down so well for me,
(though I will gather them, all that may arrive).
I plant more within myself.
A little more as I gain age and perspective,

as if there is a tiny, deep nudge of spore,
a hint of deathly patience, like a mold beginning,
that pulls upward in a clutch toward light,
and takes me up like a mother's cancer
to consume me flesh, soul, and all.

I become a lonely man
who plants no flowers, believing
they will never grow.

Through certain winters there is the living
from larders of reason and hope, and the eating
toward despair at the bottom of the cabinet.

But then with spring, I never remember it
happening that precise way.
So, I re-remember it.

I get caught up in baseball for a while.
Then forest hikes in early morning rain,
or some damn modern scheme to save everyone
in the world but who I'd really save if I could.

There is also another me who watches
a friend's unhappy wife turn unhappier still.
Football is sometimes to blame,
or just the desperate passing of time,

as in the news it's routinely reported
when another slate-grey winter man
is discovered standing empty
in his living room, alone with a sudden gun.
Oh, I can
remember how that may feel…

Did you ever wait for spring?
I mean with seeds in your mouth
and your hair a field of yellow straw
just waiting to green?
Your arms embracing birdsong and sunshine,
and you noticing the absence of long spent
adolescence and daydreams?

So have I.

Maybe then you know some part of the frenzy
when those damned flowers you planted,
you buried alive, all but embalmed, forgave,
offered up for firmly dead,
rise from their muddy grave and pollinate

Yet we sometimes plant seeds too deep,
as if hiding them or daring them to transform.
Why do I feel like writing a psalm
when I've threatened the world with making
new life out of innocent little seeds?

Creation selects among those who can wait for it.
But I am too busy focusing on next year,
impatient for the promise that hard root
will pump up into soft, urgent color,
while underneath the tender root hairs
break through the rocks
that have tortured my spade's brittle tooth.

When that happens, I am turned in a circle
and become the nimble-fingered magician
with knowing eyes,
large arms,
a muddy smile,
and a root reaching through my shoe.

POET'S JOURNEY

I swam one moonless night
        with a Sicilian fisherman.
We held our breath as we went down.
The darkness and silence were shrouds.

He taught me to probe rock cracks
with my fingers.
Octopi and Eels would slither out.
We'd hold a net with our free hand
        to catch the things making their
        escape into the Ionian Sea.
"You must let the fish come to you," he said.
Even then, I learned, you could not trust
        the net or the eel.

Returning from the tragedy
of Syracusa, Plato said the Poets lied.
        Listen, he said, to storytellers
        who speak beauty not truth.
Do not deceive yourselves
        with pleasures
perpetually re-desired.
        He implied that he gained everything
by giving up his wealth.

"Believe what you feel," said my guide,
        "easy in your palm."
Grip tight and you are left
with a handful of slime.

THE LOCAL TRIBE

I was raised in a minority family
        in the Midwest.
Well, not so much minority really
        being half Italian in neighborhoods
bristling and proud of Irish descent.
        But that half Italian made me wish
              to be like all the rest — all Irish.

My friends were all Irish all the time
        and spoke of being Celtic
            and how proud they were.

To them I was a dago.
        Really only half dago.
I did not think of my other half —
        English.
The same English who for a thousand years
made minorities of the Irish

Stay with me as this gets a little more complicated
        then hopefully, some light will shine.

Older yet, I learned about Romans.
Ah, Italians who for hundreds of years
        made minorities out of everyone they could find
        including of course, the English and the Celts.

So now, living as I do among many
American tribes, America's Celts, I see a
different perspective on all of this.

I wonder if they ever imagine
themselves to be like Irish Celts
        or are satisfied at being America's Celts.
Or maybe they wish at a chance for once
        to be the English
            or maybe even the Romans.

Maybe they would imagine being the Etruscans
      and bullying the upstart Romans
           in the time before Rome?

Actually, I wonder why they would not.

They remind me and all of us
      the importance we give our tribe.
But maybe just as much
      that we are all tribal only so far,
one half, one-quarter, one-eighth,
then the precious 64th.

The real test is perhaps
      not what we were born,
          not what we were raised,
      but the labels we wear
       like brand names and designer jeans.

It feels like standing still
      when we feel
        the need for speed.
A feeling of being valued somewhere
      distant from where we are.

Maybe we can try this:
      Being without a tribe, without
      a history that always ends sad.
A history repeated again and again
      new but forever ancient.

All our tribes, all our family
      transformed by a cause
      made into more than myth and mystery.

WEATHERING

Northern rain
        has me searching, waiting for snow.
Southern rain is storm warning.
        Eastern winds say move along
Westward wind slows us down

We see sunsets then
        Nighttime is for musing
Daylight discloses everything
        Hours are so long
But days leap and fly away

CARDINAL CENTER RIGHT

I was saved by Brahms, to my surprise,
from the eighth-grade error of a date forgotten.

I forgot, you see, the field trip to the symphony.
Now, all were ready for the bus,
all in their black jackets,
except me in a new proud scarlet shirt.

The jeers of children targeting the different,
had me in tears in the boys' room.
I was ushered to departure,
though I begged not to go.

Katy was there, witness to it all.
But the Nuns were resolute —
I would go to Severance Hall.

But Brahms saved me.
In the dark and the rows of seats,
we were all alike.

During the performance, we became invisible
and the lingering notes hung like posters
in the silences between the tones.
I learned the power of serious music and

I was conducted, like a ruby
from the anonymous pyrite, from a seat
center-right and transformed.

The crows of night
revealed the cardinal of nostalgia —
me, the modest survivor legato
became unaware of all around me.
Then, Katy took my hand.

GRAN MILONGA

> Launch of Gran Milonga
> Blaine to Bellingham passage
> March 27, 2017

It's a dance,
a gathering, as of wind
and water,
all mixing.

We launch
inviting adventure.
At sea, currents
carry us, as in the dance
the music carries us.

We turn face to face
and take a warm embrace,
we let loose the lines
to feel where melody
might climb, dip, soar
and finally settle.

HUMANS—FROM THE FELINE GUIDE

They do not climb well
nor need to. They can reach high.
They move about upraised,
exposing their tender bellies.

Their hearts are slow,
but very strong.
They are like our mothers
when not aroused.

The males do not sit
to move water and
they scrape their throats
with razor blades.

The females show affection,
make tears, and laugh with their voices
against our ribs.
They hum us their melodies.

The small ones
inevitably grow large.
They become less fun,
but grow more gentle.

They may inflict much pain
With their size and with
their mysterious tempers.
We must hear them come.

Even asleep their breath
Is a great wind.
Their eyes and nose are not strong
yet they always find our marks.

Being slow they may live
nine of our lives.

FACTORY JOB

I'd rather rob a drug store,
but I've got no appetite for a gun fight
or to shoot some working stiff or pharmacist.

I'd accept inherited money, of course,
and money found in a plain paper bag
tossed from a moving train.

It could even rain down unexplained
like food to fish in an aquarium
their gaping mouths taking in miracle flakes

of manna dropped by an incomprehensible god.
Instead, I work the night shift
assembling boxes or inspecting engine parts

or looking down the throats of mortar shells.
It makes no difference to me.
If I had more nerve or less or if my imagination

were wider or deeper, I'd do something else
and probably earn much more.
Who knows — maybe I'd be a banker

and sell mortgages to factory workers
or Chevrolets to farm labor? I'd find a way
then to stay awake all night

and worry instead about my next tax break.
I've got my friends and we go for beer
or to the all-night Denny's for burgers and fries.

We're all trying to make living worth something.
We watch the games and argue over distractions
like politics or union leaders' predictions.

We line up our children for chances
at the day shift, so we can all carry on
producing stuff and more factory jobs

for more stuff and more factory jobs.
I'll vote left or right, whoever promises benefits.
My car payment is on my mind,

and the rent can't be far behind and
my wife's ring still has installments to satisfy.
I won't worry who is wrong or right.

My ideals have taken flight, my kids need
new phones and cheap factory food, GMO'd
and certified. We live by paychecks

early light this better life, this warm factory
incubator and producer of consumer
goods of the self-satisfied style

all middle class within our mother's womb.

WEATHER REPORT

My favorite today
        is the heavy fog of the Pacific Northwest.

I love the surprise of it.
        Of all fog really, the way
        it so completely conceals
        then suddenly reveals.

But today it's the coast
        that lights me up
        as it dims the day to gray.

Surprise is in the composition of youth
        when everything is new
        and un-expected.

So, it is youth that grips us when
        in the gray and drizzle and out of nothing
        an eagle's claws suddenly reach forward
        and grasp a cedars crest. Come from nowhere
        and now there clings an eagle
        a moment, then leans into the mist and disappears.

Yet, fog can be a killer.
        Another surprise
        not so bad in the end
        and maybe a delight
        in what we so dread.

I'm walking in fog
        today again, like so many days,
        but this time toward a deep cliff,
        a ledge I must find along
        this steep and slippery trail.

It could be, will be, only one slip,
       or one step amazed out into sudden space
       so, I am watchful.
       Why do I fight surprises?

As I move along, alone in the dawn,
       a small field before the crevice
       erupts up into a gale
       of goldfinches.

Their brilliant gold and black defies the somber
       and their excited calls
       tell of their own surprise
       as we all arrive together.

And I am young a moment on their wings
       a part of the whole
       carried up
       just when I expected to fall.

TWO DAYS

One day to live this life
        and one to see a change.
Two ways to see the same faces,
the same sunrises or sunsets.

One day to explore and one to gather.
Two times we walk each path testing
        each outcome and finally accepting
        that we can never know,
        can never accept

how one day misses the important point
and one day is pointless, and another day teaches
        the point of all days.

These days—
        calendar markers,
        appointment holders,
        reservations missed,
        opportunities,
and the great days too—
        every day, tomorrow and yesterday,
my day and your day
        and no two remembered alike.

Two days: peace and war, plenty and hunger.
Two ways each going their own way
        and we carry along, going upstream or down,
one voice saying, "This way out," one saying
        "This way in."
Both determined: Don't linger halfway.
It's all in, one way or the other.

But there we stand,
> at revolution's edge, seeing
there is no one way,
> no magic path, no middle, beginning or end
> beyond the chosen beliefs.

Today or tomorrow, one day finally
> as easy as two,
> all as if planned
> in circular resolution.

One day or two days?
Two days to decide
> and everything waiting
> counting the hours, adding up
> the final days.

TAI CHI

In the mornings Tai whispers to me,
offers itself and promises small praise.
I can do this dance
as I have for 30 years,
imperfectly but with enthusiasm.
I expand as I balance.
I never watch myself, never imagine
one missed step or forgotten pose
lest it all unravels
like a ball of twine untwisted.
One small move at a time.
First finish,
then move on
breathing the universe
in 54 movements.

MANZANITA RUSH
— THE EXPLORERS

Over land, it's a long reach
to the Pacific coast from Missouri territory.
Whole seasons they labored
over mountain passes and endless plains.

They made deals along the way,
bartering beads for their way upstream
and wintering where the storms found them.
The game was virgin to their guns.

They spoke no French or Blackfoot
but their guide was true, not knowing
the gift she gave for a single footnote
in their surveyor's journal.

They came to explore and to claim
and they took it all for the forests,
for the gold, for the sod and for pride.
Destiny and Jefferson were on their side.

They had the long trek home, but first
the grey wet winter exploring beaches
of the new land they claimed.
Fool's gold puddled in their footsteps.

THE CLOCKMAKER

I am the maker of clocks
I am the machine maker
Who counts the code
of hours mysteriously turned into days.

Slowly ticking the metronome beats
a steady rhythm, as the platen presses the gyre.
The spring is tensed, ready to release
as the hour arrives plodding along.

Time is free,
but the measurement is expensive.
The price of nostalgia is bittersweet.
Predicted mathematically,

the sweep clears the shaft
the pendulum prompts movement
chimes dwindle away in distance.
The years fly away.

PASSING PIGEONS

They made the daylight sky
into midnight at noon.
Their wings created their own wind

in the roar of passage.
Who could imagine an end
to this storm?

Who saw the last of the
droppings after eons fertilizing
the great eastern oak forests?

Or the end of the forests?
The end of the sea itself
just as un-believable.

Yet there came a day and one last bird,
pulling birdshot to itself
like an inevitable magnet.

BROKEN DOWN

The tow truck driver arrives on time.
The old car is winched and we're on our way.

It feels warm in the cab beside him.
From the dark our voices emerge.

I learn he has lost his second wife to cancer.
He has it also, a legacy of two tours in 'Nam.

It is what it is, he reconciles, but
I think he drives slow to stretch the visit—

Winter nights on side roads are thin for tows.
Broken down, fixed again, I move

from break down to break down.
I repair, refresh, push on with new stories,

old stories and faces, friends, strangers,
with salesmen and store clerks. It's all about reservations

missed and made and the toil of road or rail or flight.
Travelling requires detours.

There are no straight roads to anywhere complex,
and the easy climbs are too soon downhill.

It's all fate or play in the fields of mischievous saints.
Plans not well done or the unexpected axle snap

become only something to tell.
Broken downplays well.

To live a little forward, to send a lesson
to find some shaping, a bell note

a murmur that something has changed.
A lightening strike, a tidal wave

or the last dollar not yet spent,
the I-still-give-a-damn delight

that plays so well
to this encounter.

Questions in Bottles

QUESTIONS IN A BOTTLE

I can't save you and you can't save anyone.
We are all un-saved all on our own islands

crouching at the surf, poking notes full of questions
and replies down the necks of bottles.

We set adrift our thoughts and hopes and best intentions
for other survivors to find and ponder

as they in turn pack their own bottles
with love and loneliness, deceits and demands.

We launch the gabble with the pious philosophy
and the great pretense that help is on the way.

We wade the surf, hauling in
our daily fish and our notes in bottles.

Time is on our hands. Time, time, time…
time ticking…. ticking with the surf.

We pop the corks hoping this time,
this one metaphorical and transformative time

to finally find magic and magician
and all the answers, or any answers,

even one answer, one believable answer
to even one believable question.

TRICKLE DOWN

A fine madness grows up in March
in stormed over houses, where people wait for sun.
The trees stand quiet, waiting too,
without buds. They know what is yet to come.

Spring will pull no jokes on them.
Their dull sap is puddled safe in the roots.
Their branches
hold leaves of blackbirds who scatter

like memories of autumn, twirling mad
on the breath of lion wind.
They are starved as we are.
They have fed for months on worms of snow.

This is not the spring
of maidens and shepherd pipes.
It is not a melody of Disney characters
pushing shoots up into warm life,

or churchgoers knelt
in streams of picture light.
It is not a pink rabbit
or a bed of fragile yellow blooms.

Now we live close to the street,
we become the street,
we become the windows,
we become the objects we hide or sleep behind.

We would rather still be believers
at least hoping to find some purpose.
Roads run all directions, none feel welcome.
We know about programs that we never fit.

We know about disappearing.
We don't know about reappearing.
We sleep here, because this is what we know.
We have the night, and we have the morning.

We have the memory of dreams
that still linger
in our shivering
for the promises of youth.

But our capital is spent.
We have been flushed and rehabbed
until we are empty.
Clean again, we rise up one more time.

There may be soup at the shelter lunch.
There may be a generous hand.
Perhaps a priest
with silver candle sticks will come today.

Instead, a pimp is waiting in his
pastel Cadillac.
His lady huddles in a hallway
with a ten dollar ticket.

A social worker looks away,
sees a young mother watching from
a soiled window. Hope is picking the teeth
of all their desperate decisions.

An old man passes by, leather-tied
to a black dog named Lucky.
A child on a bike peddles off another way,
and the dog turns, wanting to run.

TIME MACHINE

Perhaps we have been, or are already being
toyed with. If so — how would we know?

What more Godlike technology can man
invent than a machine to carry us

through time, to other places or the same,
but forward or back.

What can we ever do to more
leverage all history and all futures,

to modify all outcomes,
and to make everything

forever different than it would
otherwise have been.

It's an interesting process. Imagine visiting
a Dallas warehouse on November 22, 1963,

and just for an instant deflecting
that man's attention to his aim?

That's just a start.
It doesn't have to be big works

to matter. The smallest adjustments
will ripple through all eternity.

A fly not caught in a swallow's flight
Inevitably changes all futures.

Titanic's lookout not forgetting his binoculars.
Caesar learning of Brutus' change of heart…

Hamlet's deciding to be, or not.
It's endless this speculation

as difficult to fill as infinity,
or as limitless as space.

Can even God tinker with time travel?
Can God do it over or better this time?

If time travel is ever to be invented
then it already is.

Are we the products
of a time traveler's tinkering?

Did Lucy turn right or left
on her way out of the savannah,

at a time traveler's suggestion?
We will never know, and there is

no way to imagine the arena of
difference it could all mean.

But maybe an idea is all it takes.
You being here with me, right now.

You considering my words
and bending your imagination

with me for just this moment.
Together, we change everything.

NOTRE-DAME DE PARIS

The grand edifice floats in memory,
      amid clouds of curiosity and adulation,
      a symbol beyond replication.

In times when bonded labor is unavailable,
we must do the rebuilding ourselves,
empty our pockets and bank accounts,
sully the heavy stones block-by-block.

All to provide another 500 years of tourists
to wonder at the why of our philanthropy.
These are our times, our chance
to send imagination on a millennial journey.

So yet again the choirs will sing,
      the great bourdon Emmanuel will ring.
The aged mysteries we'll keep vaulted,
      but the spire will straighten our wills.

Out of ruins we will point a single modern finger
      To the sky, to stars, to God, pretending we
           know the unimaginable future.

BAPTISM

Then,
        beside the river, on his calloused knees,
        knelt the prophet
        with an ocean in his hands.

        With skilled eyes ablaze and seraphim,
        he grappled with will,
        bleeding it clean of guilt,
        washing it among the marbled stones
        and eddies of swirling, translucent silt.

        Even the dancers took hold
        as the singers accompanied
        The water, they could boil.

Until,
        not even a blank page resembled us,
        written upon, then erased;
        even our mothers' cries at her womb
        would not disclose the smallest
        meaningful trace.

For,
        we never escaped from forgiveness
        with its divine implications,
        having emerged wrapped in the rags
        of original sin, denying the strong
        resemblance to innocence.

So,
        it took ceremonies for which
        we never volunteered,
        the salt on our tongues,
        and the cry of salvation
        poured upon our foreheads
        through our brains, unbelieving,
        to reveal to us
        the dark mark we carry.
        Thus, are the fingers
        pressed upon us,
        forgiving in advance,
        the prophecy of sin.

HOW WOULD I PAINT?

W/out eyes:
    I would be still. I would practice.
    Not a breath. The wind and my heart would slow.
    Time would not wait, and I would feel it go.
    Then, finally, the colors would begin

W/out paint:
    It is not easy without paint. But
    There is always paint. If I will dig
    Deep enough, If I will steal,
    If I will open veins with fingernails,
    I would paint

W/out reason:
    I would turn bright eyes and my remaining ear
    Toward morning light. I would pose in my chair,
    Take up the heavy, impressionable paint,
    And stare deeply into a mirror.

W/out arms:
    I would concentrate on birds and fish.
    Snakes, perhaps.

W/out time:
    Even on that wide water,
    Even without a sound,
    It is hard to believe I could not trace
    One quick finger in the rising tide.

THE SMILE

I often stop in my garden
to praise my patient and silent Buddha.

I pat his round head
and rub his watermelon-shaped belly.

He smiles back at me.
No god responds, no lightning strikes

and no salvation manifests
in unpulled dandelions

or yellowjackets
hungry for prey.

I ask for nothing.
Nothing comes in reply.

Role Play

CURRENT AFFAIRS

Someone put another coin in the slot
        sending the merry-go-carousel
        around another revolution.

Some things grow too large,
        defying attempted comprehension
        but with compelling reason.

We are submerged in undertow
        of ridiculous claims repeated
        and repeated into fake facts.

We begin real conversation
        only if we finally agree
        on vocabulary and definition.

We need the drudgery of agreement
        or it all becomes a hypnotism
        of gyrations, a hammering

of terms and accusations like iron spikes
        with the passion of blind belief
        demanding equal claim with hard science.

Then the only card in the deck
        we can still recognize is the joker
        wearing a transparent smirk

in his deception of an honored game.
        There is the tyrant's invitation to fall
        like supplicants to our knees

among the building blocks scattered about.
        Once there was a solid plan
but it did not become a habit.

BLACK OR WHITE

When everything rides,
with the bet on everything,
being right
will be important.

Being sure
feels safe.
Just ask the builders of bridges
or spaceships.

It seems like an easy world
where everything is black or white,
yes or no.
Nothing is gray,
and nothing is in color.
Everything only right or wrong.

Being correct requires only
some definition.
An understanding of time shifts,
between generations,
with perspective.

Righteousness feels strong.
But the shift is quick.
So very sure,
we're made fools of by time.

We step proudly,
already in free fall.

SAFETY

So, we need to be safe—
and these ones are a danger;
they know what we must know—
Knowledge is power
regardless of how obtained.
It is good sense to interrogate
the suspects
and re-interrogate the convicts.
It is in the holy name of safety
that we must play this unsavory game.
It is their fault for knowing
what we must learn.
Their fault we must drag it from them
Even if with patience, they'd tell us anyway.

We need to decide, of course
who is suspect
Not necessarily suspect of What—
only who.
Then for What we can wait
as we whittle them down,
stretch them out, water or shock,
their simple screams soundproofed
and their sobs ignored as trickery.

We'll need to decide who decides;
Who is suspect and who is cleared.
But for safety, the net must be fine meshed
and widely cast.
For safety it is better that none slip through.
Many suspects will be cleared;
it's always the way, but for safety we
can't let anyone think we're the fools,
that we are not the ones in power.

We'll work through the maze
of Who, Where and When
as we dutifully make way to safe caves
where we can hoard all we have learned
and build barricades to separate
the safe and sane from all the others.
Let the spirituals argue over degrees.
We'll keep them safe also
until they are on the lists then by and by.

And care must be used in selection
of interrogators. Thick skins needed,
pride in their work, managing fear
and administering pain
in the name of safety; pride in their belief
they do their work for the greater good.
We should be so lucky with our volunteers —
train them well.
These will be the ones
who will marry our daughters.

THE SKY IS FALLING

The sky is falling. I believe the sky is falling. I accept this belief, that the sky is being pulled down by gravity. The sky is falling despite everything telling us that such a thing is not possible. The sky falls because I believe it falls. Here it comes now. I can feel it pressing down on us. I love believing it is pressing down, falling down upon us. I need this believing, this utter certainty, which is my belief the sky is falling.

I was told the sky is falling, so I believe it. Someone told me. Someone wrote it in a book. The President makes it an order, that the sky is falling, so I must believe it. Because it is the truth, they said, that the sky is falling and it is beyond question that it is almost here, falling on us, pressing us into the earth like tiny seeds. We are told it is the sky and that is good enough. No more reason is given. No more reason to complicate our belief. No more reason to wonder why, or when, or how.

Here it comes, so take comfort, take cover. Take your time, your mind and take argument with you. I'm resolved. It's all coming down. I believe it is almost here. Because I am correct you know. I was told and now I'm telling you. It was written and now I'm writing you. You must believe it too. It's better. It's the law. It's a rule. Written here. All that matters is belief. And belief there is a sky.

DIALOGUE

Can we possibly make these words tidy?
Perhaps make them ring with the crystal of rhyme?
Can we flow in meter and make the apostrophe

fit in just so? Can we make any of it
more meaningful than ink on paper
or magnets on pixel?

It's all floating in cartoon thought
like hidden meaning in a cloud,
and if not that, then it's falling snow

or the wind whistling past our earbud.
A word almost heard, a great idea
almost comprehended.

EVERYDAY JUSTICE

We save daylight in our fists
Our anger grows out of colors
Red for pain, black for evil
White is for indifference
Gold is the price to depart

Invisible are the children
The sound is children's laughter
Becoming their broken hearts

Patience for justice
feels like a game
with one way participation.
Names for winners are created and texted
The state media obscures the obituaries
The social media twists popular fictions.
Every theory gets minutes of credibility
Then lifetimes of scorn.

Is this how the pharaohs faced discontent?
Put the chain gangs to work, hauling stone
Making commerce the protected class.

No wonder the Jesus turned
Money lenders and shop keepers out.
No wonder kristalnacht was an insult
pivoting the world to Hiroshima.

We don't know
the definition of justice,
but like a coat of mail or a drape of ermine,
we can feel the difference.

FIXING THE SYSTEM

This work requires us
to get inside
where the guts are packed.
Where the heat from the organic
stimulus creates all our sweat.

Begin there to pull out
all the plumbing.
Take a first screw
Then a rivet.
Tug out some wires.

One hand pulls right
The other yanks to the left.
Both are pretending
knowing where it all ends,
acting it out, with determination.

Soon it all begins
to fall apart.
We overdo it,
as we always do.

Some call the process improvement
While others will scream revolution.

We work through beta tests,
approvals, rejections, and exhaustion
from explaining every step.

We have to deal with all the parts
that no longer fit.
And with the parts we forgot.

Finally, we feel complete.
Just in time to realize
It is time to start over again.

ADDICTED TO SALVATION

We treasure the deep sigh of satisfaction,
the warmth in our being, or the joy of
playing again with unblessed die.

We know it's all a gamble
with smoke or spirit, with colors
or dissolved granules so easily injected

direct to the highway of our heart and
the repository of the mind.
There is power in filling out our hollow shell.

We're victims too, but in charge
of our own tortures. We are the hooded priests,
the executioners, and so

we're addicted to the illusion of knowing,
of believing, and self-deceiving that
we are our own masters.

We pretend the hard decisions,
including the minor chord, the false note
that making any changes,

taking a new direction, is entirely
an original idea
within our own control.

GOD BLESS

I like best the veterans with their dogs
when I come to them standing at a corner.
I know the dog may be just for marketing,
But still I buy a can of Canine Stew
to give to the vet as I pass by.

Here was a cardboard sign unlike the others
held by the homeless, the veterans, the hungry
and unlucky in a country filling up
with the homeless, the hungry and the veterans
on the corners all across the country.

This lone man held my favorite sign.
He looked me straight in the eye,
earning respect for honesty and its attendants
of creativity and even humor,
especially when unexpected.

This sign was the winner.
"I promise to pay your generosity forward."
I unloaded my wallet, mostly singles,
to reward this image of my dollars floating
hand to hand, going forward again and again.

His "thanks" would have been enough.
He could save for himself his goodbye hope.
"God bless" he said, the ultimate generosity.
Please pay that forward also, I wish,
and take good care of the dog.

THE PERFECT POEM

The perfect poem will not depend
On meter or rhyme

The perfect poem will transcend
Poetic artifice and simple design

The perfect poem will arrive complete
Though not at first appear so

The perfect poem will touch all hearts
And reside within all minds.

The perfect poem will emerge as a sculptor
Uses a chisel slowly revealing their work.

The perfect poem can speak aloud
Not requiring paper or pen or printing

The perfect poem will not wake me at 2 am
With one more idea or correction.

The perfect poem will live within
Perpetually transforming itself and us.

The perfect poem
Will be worth waiting for.

The perfect poem
will be the next poem.

Star Trails

HEAVEN

Name it here
or name it there

If it's anywhere,
it's everywhere.

We're already in infinity —
where else could it be?

It can't be something that we do.
If it's anyone – it's you.

Perhaps it's a place eternally silent
with the righteous forever private.

There may be no dividing line
with now or never all the same in time.

Stars without anger or mercy.
There will be no memory.

HELL

A place that only works
When we believe in it.
Then works so well
We must forever ignore it.

PURGATORY

Where are we?
This constant wonder
Where we are and when.
How did it come to this?
Where this will go
Is impossible to measure.
Will there ever be an end?
How did this start?
And inevitably, the unanswerable
Question of why.

KATABATIC

Anything can come out of this night.
The movement of wind is a saw
      picking along my shingles,
      leaning on my windows.

Each of its insistent possibilities presses
      loud voices into the hollows of my spine
reminding me of root cellar safety while
      teasing with sarcastic bells of laughter.

      There's a pressure in this invisible posture.
Wind will be what it makes of itself.
      Yet wind is thoughtless, or its own idea.
In darkness, its invisible voice is magnified.

This wind is a great inhalation
      sucking like a yawn through the trees,
      pulling into a tenseness,
      like an enormous contraction.

It's got me tight, waiting out
      the first vortex to crash back,
      a destructive conception
      twisting the worst of the night into a howl

      and spitting it back as teeth.
This night feels perpetual.
Like two invisibilities moving
      within each other.

>   Like a line of sight
>   through the pit of an eye.
> Anemoi a transparent witness,
>   It has got me probing to find.

Then, against the panes the wind finally eases.
Not beaten; one cannot beat a spirit.
It sobs restlessly in my rose bushes.
      Brittle brambles scratch against the slats.

This wind falls out of the mountains,
      moves over any water, bends grassy plains
      as it comes to me. In the wildness of space,
      it is a freedom voice that demands
      it is wilder than me.

For all the nights,
      as long as this gale moves, I will listen.
To sleep now,
      I need the wind to howl.

Or to lie in silence.
      Breathless.

RIPPLING

> In all of creation there exists only 2 things:
> substance and lack of substance
> —Spinoza

It seems we can't stir up
even
a single molecule without it jostling
the molecule next to it,
and then the next,
like infinite dominoes
marching off to the edge of space.

There may be some meaning in this,
or we want it implied.
Yet perhaps space has no edge,
it being the opposite of a world,
bent in waves, curved around over us.

All this is enough to have us careful
where we step, or what we say.
Who knows where a thing will go.

We come down this way
a ripple in ourselves, making waves
like a mayfly dimpling a still pond.
Inevitable these echoes,
like a beginning and end,
if there is one.

There is this utter realization:
All our loving whispers, all our big deals,
all our rosary beads injection-molded,
all our prayer flags fluttering credos,

all our judges' mallets pounding,
all our decisions and destinations,
all the missed and made connections,
all the bullets fired.

The babies cry. The mothers cry.

Everything,

makes its way back home.

It's a long way, but certain
to arrive in time carrying
a suitcase or computer
in which are packed the unintelligible
installation instructions

and a user's manual for yesterdays
wind-up alarm clock,
following a map
      of Everywhere

      but without an X-marked spot

      for "You-Are-Here".

STAR TRAILS

Within the bloom of elliptical universe
I am scaling for that part of petal
      that is my Genesis

while stars glare by, uninvolved with us.
My clock ticks solid metal notes in my mind,
      reminds me it exists.
.
The dog pants upon my hand,
      the one unbent around this pen.
The cat turns its yellow eyes on me.

So, there is destiny in us.
A lonely thing to own.
 Can I give it back?

This curse of Cain that sent us
      to a thousand Buchenwalds
      and Waterloos?

Clock, grind me wheat.
Dog, pant a melody
Cat, where are you in those yellow eyes?

Are not meteors planets smaller than we,
ripping through voids until we come by
      with our sphere-meshed nets
capturing them to burn and die?
      So, who are we then, friend?
Man who thinks, clock that breathes,

a dog, a cat to wander through
      leaving moon dust where we sleep.
Ride this dream with me,

man who ticks a metal note,
>	where clocks mark the arc of the sun,
>	amid the sane and meaningful stars,

>	diffused by whatever Gods weaned us,
>	to measure the beats of the clock.

While a dog waits for love,

>	and a cat simply waits.

So, let us follow celestial tales.
Run our fingers

>	along star trails blazed
>	 in meteor skies too far to reach.

Too far for casual comprehension.

Clock, I tick to you, not for you.
Dog, cat, go to sleep.
We are not going home — we are there.

COLOR RISING

I saw October's dead leaves
rise up in a sudden breeze,

like autumn
going back to the trees.

I saw leaves depart the earth.
I saw them leave,

flashing bright nostalgia
for summer's green.

Leaves became light,
like forests in flight.

Dead leaves flew up
to the arms of their creators.

I saw leaves pantomime
belief in miracles.

GALILEO GALILEI

Always turn the moons
      on axis Jupiter
      for the glass

to hold in thirty power,
      focused on celestial beings
      and inward, upon the new ideas

of cannon balls racing grapes
      in fall proving both may pass
the canon law they displace.

Unburned stakes so kindled
      arouse flames
      from narrow-minded inquisitors

upon the old man's claims.
This world, uncentered,
arcs a solar halo proved on charts.

But his too full eyes went blind
      on sights the holy philosophers
      claimed he could not find.

SIBLINGS

MERCURY
    So fortunate
    the sun is so large

    But lonely to the core
    Too close to the center

VENUS
    Nothing
    is more mysterious

    Anything
    could be down there

EARTH
    All the precious colors
    and so much

    alive on the land
    alive in the sea

MARS
    Feels like our past
    or our future

    There are secrets
    never to be told

SATURN
    So much less
    than it appears

    Bringer of age and drama
    singer of ancient songs

JUPITER
    A name to admire
    A reputation beyond reach

    Strength it says, but more:
    Divinity

NEPTUNE
    The vast storms
    say "sea", say beware

    Ruler of the deep
    ocean of stars

URANUS
    Like a Greek god
    of the sky

    Classical, but sly
    Nothing more says "Magician"

YOUR DUST

Morning sunlight reveals
What is left behind
I stir the room
By walking through
Everything is rearranged
But every bit remains

MOONRISE

There is a silent splendor
        as the moon rolls into view.
For a long moment we study her.
Now, after all we have been through, we can see
that we ride on a dust mote
within clouds of dust motes.

It is here now, this evolution,
as evening exposes the underbelly of the stars.
No longer a matter of vague beliefs,
we inherit centuries of thought
        enabled by technology,
            with the compression of prisms and ground glass
expanded from science into logic.

These are droplets of information
        measured into our literal imaginations.
Like a parade of Eons,
        time itself in its lonely delight
carried to us in the rolling
        of our little orb.
We're stumbling through the night.
But we rise from our falls, and there
        our dignity is offered.

There is the chance we have it wrong, of course.
        This is the nature of belief.
But we act with utter certainty.
We may sneer at contrary opinions
        with the only act we know.

And in ten centuries,
        that generation may laugh back at us
as we laugh back our own hallway of years.
And then – will we still need God to love us?
To make us the most precious
        of all creations?

We adapt and survive.
We believe in forever, but we do not
        trust ourselves.
            Well, with our history…

But we get emergences. Breakouts.
A reason for Reason,
        or a surprise of peace.
Being hopeful; we show both our faces.
Though fearful; we can be honest
        believing as we do the theory
            "too much to lose" will make us safe.
Then we lose it all just the same.
As we knew we would.

Our certainty becomes uncomfortable
        Like bad fitting shoes
So, we choose the comedy, not in error,
        but in will and wish and hope.
We lift desperate prayers
like tons of butterflies.

And you — if you read still —
        Do you find the intersections of you and I?
Can you imagine the crumbs of perspective?
        and envelopment, of first one truth
        then the next, and again the next?

And can you also imagine time
        playing another of its subtle games?
Of infinitely larger and smaller universes
        all while we are passing by,
stirring the dust in unused rooms and hallways.
All the galaxies set in motion
        to settle where they may.

MOONLIGHT

… comes unannounced through the shadows
of clouds and pours itself into trees
filling dark spaces between limbs and leaves

… has heat turned low
that ricochets on hard frost or snow
and glitters on dancing waves.

… shows brightest when it has the least to give.
Reveals what night would leave concealed
in tones of skeletal pale

… is messenger and traveler of Earth's dusk,
is envoy of the oceanic magnet in its perfect arc
and the only bridle of the restless sea

…Moonlight leaves in silence
as our cold sister departs
her pockets filled with our dreams.

THE AMBERED PHOENIX

My back placed against the wind,
my face toward departing light,

      I waited for you.

The ocean coughed against
mountains made of sand.

      The planet pivoted and slipped.

I found you in darkness,
a small star in a lonely ebony frame.

      You were there.

Your presence reached across great space
and placed delicate fingers against my skin.

      You knew my only possession, my name.

I placed you in amber
before your image could fade.

      Your wings of flame now carry us both.

Your brightness to persevere
and your memory forever remain.

GIVE US YOUR POOR

We will give them
        Waiting lines
        Broken hopes
        Lost children
        Tear gas
        Rubber bullets
        Acrylic shields
        Permanent walls
        Face masks
        Hard batons
        Deportation
We will give them what we can

The Border

AT THE BORDER

There is this place,
then another place,
but we own no place.

We stand in lines,
that end at mountains
or seas we cannot cross,
cities that swallow us whole.

At the border we find walls,
instead of Christians,
questions at answers
and bright tents pretend as shelter.

We are locked behind doors.
Caged in waiting rooms.
Children are herded to buses
Crying our ancient lament

All our meager testaments
are blowing in the wind.

PASSAGES

Time is not slow
Time is not fast
We are the measure
Memories make us victims
Dreams defy reality
As we wonder what to make of it

SONRIENDO

The children stand
        at the border, smiling their hope,
        crying their memories
of being born poor and crowded and then sent
        from their families, from their homes
        on this lonely desperate trek.

They look at land
        they do not understand.
Some wear a cheap pack
but others have only a paper sack
carrying maybe worn, used socks and
perhaps two water bottles,
        one empty, one half full,
        and they give thanks for their wealth.

Border agents and the National Guard stand
        with rifles at ready
        and eyes trained to see
        everything. They comprehend nothing.

The children share the last bottle of water
        and their last pesos for a few
        thin tortillas.
        They count the grimy coins out equally
        between rich and poor.
                No one begs for more.

Inevitably,
> the children melt into the sand,
> vibrate away into the heat,
leaving their small sacks
> and tiny barefoot tracks.
They disappear
> these desperate ones.
Some go north,
Some slip sideways, and others
> evaporate, never to be recognized.

They send their hopes
> over the border, blessing the guards
> blessing the land, blessing the promises
>> on which they lived.

The black crows, always present,
> take wing and scream their insults
> like a haunting refrain.
The black crows
> have become the children
> have become the dreams
> and remain when all else is gone.

The children's dark eyes
> Practiced ojos en el suelo
remain in spirit also.

This is ours
        think the guards
                as they clean their guns.
They have stood their ground.
        They count mile markers back
        to all their homes and origins and
ahead to what can only be their duty
in this home of the free,
land of the brave.

HOME OF THE BRAVE

>For Sophie Scholl
>And the White Rose

Freedom can be an opinion,
       a satisfaction where nothing is really free.
Everyone is free, it seems, until
       a mysterious car rolls to a midnight stop
       before their house.

Bravery is circumstantial sometimes.
       We are all brave with a handgun in the glove box.
Bluster becomes style.
Bumper stickers swear us in for pride.

So why all the fear in the Home of the Brave?

All the armies of the world could not subdue
100 million Americans with their deer rifles.

Jefferson would nod, Napoleon would agree.
Plato wrote down Socrates' plan,
       and we all live the script
       though we have forgotten our lines.

Everyone's a hero in a fighter plane,
       but caskets come home at night
             and in private.

So, let us think of courage modeled
        by a nameless student standing in the rain
        with a column of tanks at his chin.

Brave we are, distant from the stories,
        distant from the pain,
challenged to recall the White Rose,
        its head off at the stem,
                while petals of blood
                drop like leaflets
        crossing the red-rising moon.

Now mothers and sisters march in our streets
        without guns or purchased courage.
        They fear police more than rioters.
        They fear militias more than crime.
Sorry for them, sorry for us.

We are staring at our tiny screens
        and smokescreens of gas
searching for heroes.
        We hope they are next to us.

Who lives here now,
        in this home of the brave?
We live here.

ABOUT THE AUTHOR

David found poetry in his life while a young single father. After his tour in the U.S. army, he enjoyed working toward his education, starting a career, as well as hiking and fishing with his son.

Poetry was an important companion as an outlet for his creative personality. He has carried his love of poetry alongside him in journeys across continents. David has enjoyed a robust life of travel, education, and adventure. He has garnered important life lessons from each interesting, and sometimes dangerous situation.

David has recently been a tango instructor, leading dance tours, while enjoying travel with his wife, Celie, and their two noisy dogs. He is currently working on his next volume of poems.

www.ingramcontent.com/pod-product-compliance
Lightning Source LLC
Chambersburg PA
CBHW071359290426

44108CB00014B/1608